the little book of
BEST FRIENDS

the little book of

BEST FRIENDS

Raymond Glynne

ARCTURUS

PICTURE ACKNOWLEDGEMENTS

Ardea: 6, 10, 12, 21, 23, 41, 46, 49, 53, 63, 65, 76, 80, 88, 91, 93.

Corbis: 7, 60, 85.

Creative Image Library: 82.

Empics: 28, 32, 48, 56, 64, 73, 83, 95, 96.

FLPA: 11, 59.

Getty: 29, 31, 33, 39, 43, 51, 54, 77.

Image Bank: 78, 86.

Nature Picture Library: 9, 13, 20, 26, 27, 34, 35, 36, 37, 40, 42, 44, 45, 47, 50, 57, 58, 61, 66, 79, 81, 84, 90.

Press Association: 70.

Photoshot: 14, 15, 16, 19, 62, 67, 74, 75, 94.

Robert Harding: 17, 22, 52, 68.

RSPB: 89.

Shutterstock: 8, 18, 24, 55, 69, 71, 87, 92.

Superstock: 25, 30, 38, 72.

ARCTURUS

This edition published in 2012 by Arcturus Publishing Limited
26/27 Bickels Yard, 151–153 Bermondsey Street,
London SE1 3HA

Copyright © 2010 Arcturus Publishing Limited

ISBN: 978-1-84837-760-8
AD001672EN

Printed in China

Companionship is what makes life worth living – the time spent in the company of our best friends, playing, gossiping, laughing, or simply side by side, so comfortable with each other there's no need to fill the silences.

Best friends are our boundless source of wisdom. They give us the reassurance we seek, the advice we solicit, and the truths we need to hear. They're brutally honest and they see through all our follies. Who needs 'em?

Quite simply, we all do. Because, no matter what, they love us, and we love them, in a way we just can't do without.

Best friends are always comfortable with each other...

They don't mind being used as a pillow...

Or a mattress…

Or simply somewhere to rest a sleepy head…

And they're there to share those special occasions...

Best friends take care of each other...

They know how to cheer each other up...

They reach the parts that others can't...

They protect one another's sensitivities…

And always offer a helping hand…

Best friends are always quick to share...

They share tasks...

They share their toys...

And their living space...

Even when there's barely enough room for one...

When best friends get together, watch out!...

Three is a powerful number…

An attractive package…

Trios love nothing more than a lunchtime chat...

Or a sideways whisper…

Best friends tell each other everything...

They share their secrets…

Their anxieties...

The latest news…

And their mischief…

Best friends offer each other protection…

A consoling arm around the shoulder...

They make you feel less alone...

They'll hold your hand...

And reach out to you in times of need…

Best friends always back each other up...

They present a united front...

They admire each other...

And support each other...

Even when the going gets tough…

Best friends are the best source of advice…

They keep your feet on the ground...

They help to keep things in proportion…

They'll come after you for a quiet word...

And talk you round when times are hard…

Best friends share a sense of humour…

They tell each other bad jokes...

Do silly impressions…

And once the laughter starts…

It's hard to stop…

Best friends love to go walking…

It's a chance to put the world to rights...

Catch up on the gossip...

Get lost in thought...

Or just get physical…

Best friends love to let off steam...

They're great at making their own fun...

They play sardines…

Give each other piggybacks…

And they love to spring surprises…

When the playing's done, best friends hit the hay...

They just have to crash…

Sleepovers are great fun...

It's fun to stay awake and swap stories…

But sometimes they can't help but doze off…

Sometimes best friends fall out...

A frosty silence develops…

Some refuse to confront the problem...

While others opt for the direct approach...

But the best thing about breaking up is making up...

Best friends can be mischievous at times…

They love a good prank...

But they always show tolerance...

Patience beyond the call of duty…

And absolute trust…

Best friends can sit and talk for hours...

Sharing their interests…

Pondering the meaning of life...

Enjoying the scenery...

Generally taking it easy...

Best friends see things from the same perspective…

They instinctively lean the same way...

Or balance each other out...

They dress alike…

And enjoy just hanging out together...

But through it all best friends are inseparable…

They're birds of a feather…

Whatever their hopes and dreams…

They always return to old haunts…

And stick together through thick and thin…

And when it comes to showing their feelings…

Best friends don't hold back...

Because friendship is unconditional…

And wholehearted…

And it can overcome anything at all…